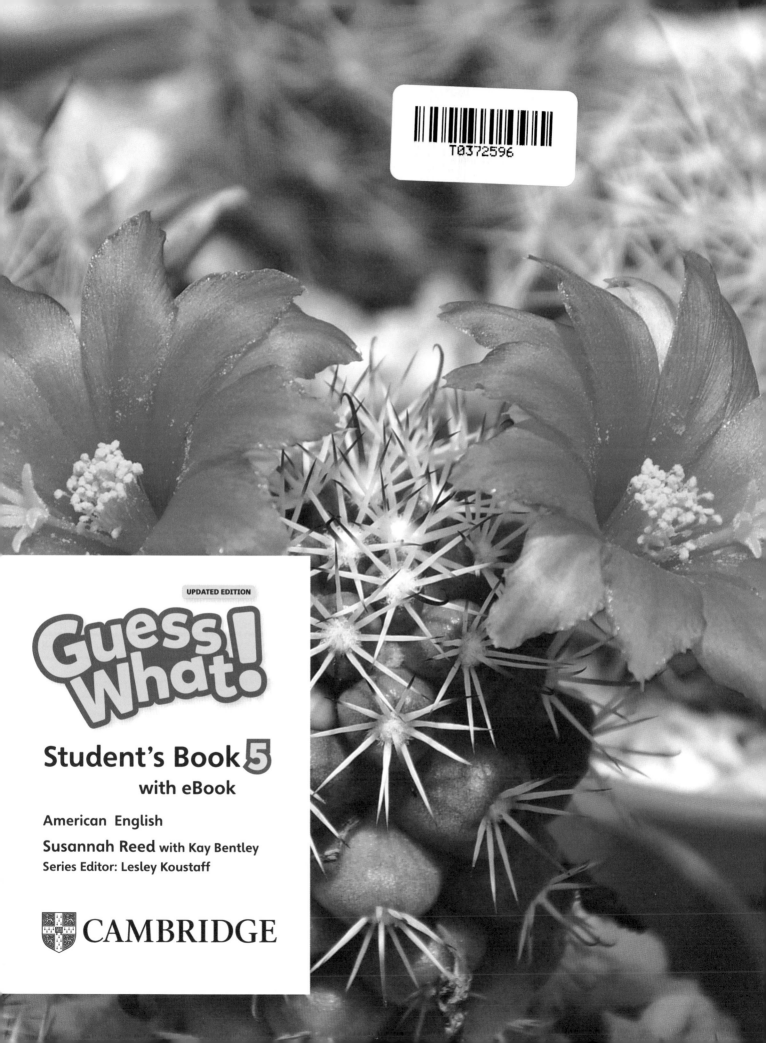

UPDATED EDITION

# Guess What!

## Student's Book 5
### with eBook

American English

**Susannah Reed** with **Kay Bentley**
Series Editor: Lesley Koustaff

**CAMBRIDGE**

# Contents

# Around the world

Look!

**1**  Listen and look.

**2**  Listen and repeat. Then match.

**1**

**2**

**3**

**4**

**5**

**6**

**7**

**8**

**9**

**10**

a Brazil    b China    c Colombia    d France    e Italy    f Mexico
g Russia    h Spain    i the United Kingdom    j the United States

**3**   **Listen and answer the questions. Then practice with a friend.**

Which country has a yellow, blue, and red flag?        Colombia!

**4**  **Which countries do you want to visit? Ask and answer.**

## 5 🎧 0.04 Read and listen.

Jules and Denis: We're from France.

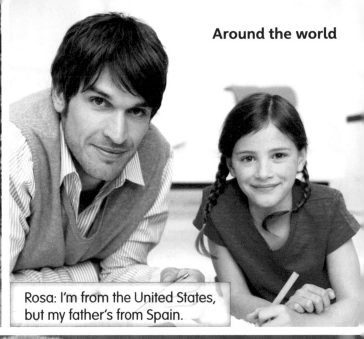

Rosa: I'm from the United States, but my father's from Spain.

Maria: I'm from Brazil.

Anton: I'm from Russia.

**Focus**

Where are you from?
I'm from the
United States.
Is he from France?
Yes, he is.
No, he isn't.

## 6 Match the questions and answers. Then ask and answer.

1 Where is Rosa from?
2 Where are Jules and Denis from?
3 Is Maria from Brazil?
4 Is Anton from Italy?
5 Where is Rosa's father from?

a He's from Spain.
b No, he isn't. He's from Russia.
c They're from France.
d She's from the United States.
e Yes, she is.

## 7 My World Answer the questions. Then ask a friend.

Where are you from?
Where are your friends from?

Where are your parents from?
Where are your grandparents from?

## 8 🎧 0.05 Go to page 102. Listen and repeat the chant.

→ Workbook page 5     Grammar

Grammar fun!
▶

7

**When is Carla's birthday? Listen and choose.**

a  in February   b  in April   c  in August

**10** **Listen again and practice.**

**Alex:** When's your birthday, Carla?
**Carla:** On April 24th.
**Alex:** So is mine! When were you born?
**Carla:** I was born in 2006. On April 24th, 2006.
**Alex:** Oh! I was born in 2006, too!
**Carla:** Where were you born?
**Alex:** I was born in the United Kingdom. What about you?
**Carla:** I was born in Spain.

**11** **Read about the children.
Then ask and answer.**

**Emma**
**Date of birth:**
June 2nd, 2005
**Place of birth:**
the United States

**Alex**
**Date of birth:**
April 24th, 2006
**Place of birth:**
the United Kingdom

**Carla**
**Date of birth:**
April 24th, 2006
**Place of birth:**
Spain

**Pedro**
**Date of birth:**
January 31st, 2005
**Place of birth:**
Brazil

When was Alex born?        On April 24th, 2006.

Where was he born?        He was born in the United Kingdom.

## Say it!

**12** **How many syllables are there in each word? Listen, count, and repeat.**

**Spain**     **birth**-day     Oc-**to**-ber

**1**

WORLD QUIZ
How many questions can you answer?

A PRIZE FOR THE WINNERS!

Hey, Ruby, look at this!

It sounds fun! Let's take the quiz together!

**2**

What's the first question, Jack?

Which city in Colombia has a flower festival?

**3**

My pen pal, Sofia, is from Colombia! We can email her.

OK, let's go to the reading room.

**4**

Where is everyone?

This isn't the reading room!

**5**

Listen to this!

To win the quiz,
Let's play a game.
Answer the questions,
And come home again.

START

**6**

What should we do?

Let's play the game. We want to win the quiz!

**7**

What's happening?

**8**

Value: Try new things　　**9**

# Skills: *Listening and speaking*

**Let's start!** What do people do at festivals?

**14**  Where are these festivals? Listen and match.

a Brazil   b China   c Spain   d the United Kingdom   e the United States

**1**

Bonfire Night, Lewes

**2**

Feria, Seville

**3**

New Year, Shanghai

**4**

Carnival, Rio de Janeiro

**5**

Independence Day, New York

**15**  Listen again and say the missing words.
1 Bonfire Night is on            5th.
2 Feria is always in            .
3 Chinese New Year is in            or            .
4 The Carnival in Rio de Janeiro starts on a            .
5 Independence Day is on            4th.

**16**   Plan a tour of some festivals.

Which festivals would you like to go to?        I'd like to go to …

Where are they?        The … is in …

# Skills: *Reading and writing*

 **Look below!** **What does Kiara want to be?**

**17** (0.12) **Read and listen.**

Kiara is eleven years old, and she's from Moscow in Russia. Kiara wants to be a dancer. She goes to dance classes every week. She wants to dance at the Russian Winter Festival.

The Russian Winter Festival takes place every year in Moscow, in December and January.

Moscow is very cold in the winter, and there's a lot of snow. There are a lot of fun activities at the festival. You can go on a troika ride through the snow. Or you can go ice-skating in the city. There are also lots of beautiful snow sculptures.

At night, you can watch the fireworks. Or you can go and see a show with traditional singers and dancers. Look out for Kiara!

**18** **Read again and correct the sentences.**

1   Moscow is in China.
2   Kiara wants to be an artist.
3   The Winter Festival is in November and January.
4   It's hot in the winter in Russia.
5   You can go swimming in the city.
6   You can watch fireworks in the morning.

Moscow isn't in China.    It's in Russia.

**Your turn!**

Think of a festival you enjoy.
When is it?
Which country is it in?
What can you see there?
What can you do there?

**Now write about it in your notebook.**

# What are mosaics made of?

# 1 🎧 0.13 Listen and repeat.

tiles

marble

ceramic

glue

# 2 CLIL ▶ Watch the video.

# 3 🎧 0.14 Read and listen.

There are lots of different mosaics in countries around the world. Mosaics are made of many small tiles. These tiles are different shapes and colors, and are made of ceramic, glass, paper, or stones, like marble.

Artists put glue on mosaic tiles and then make pictures or patterns with them. Sometimes artists glue the tiles onto cardboard first, then stick the cardboard with the mosaics onto walls, floors, and roofs.

In the past, mosaics in Roman gardens and baths were made of round stones or shells. Today, artists make mosaics for places like train stations and shopping malls to make them look beautiful.

**Guess What!**
In Spain, some artists used spoons, forks, and knives in mosaics.

**Let's collaborate!**

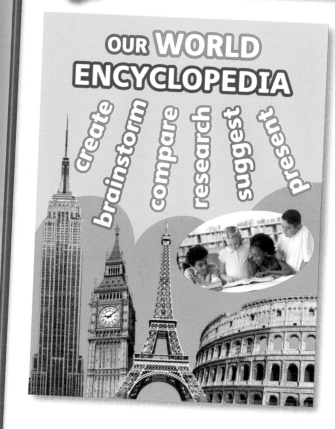

OUR WORLD ENCYCLOPEDIA

create brainstorm compare research suggest present

# 4 Answer the questions.

1 What kind of art has many small tiles?
2 What can the tiles be made of?
3 Where were there very old mosaic floors?
4 Why do artists make mosaics today?

# 5 Where would you put a mosaic in your school?

→ Workbook page 10

CLIL: Art

# 1 Family and pets

Look!

Guess What!

**1** 🎧 1.01 **Listen and look.**

**2** 🎧 1.02 **Listen and repeat. Then match.**

**1** my grandparents

**2** my aunt

**3** my parents

**4** my uncle

**5** my sister

**6** my brother

**7** my cousin

**8** my best friend

**9** my kitten

**10** my puppy

---

**a** artistic  **b** smart  **c** friendly  **d** funny  **e** hardworking
**f** kind  **g** naughty  **h** shy  **i** sporty  **j** talkative

---

**3** 🎧 1.03 (Think) **Listen and guess who. Then practice with a friend.**

They're friendly.    They're Alex's grandparents!

**4** (My World) **What is your family like? Ask and answer.**

**5** **Read and listen.**

**Focus**

My dog is smarter than my cat.
My brother is more hardworking than my sister.

I'm more talkative than my cousin,
She's shyer than me.
And I'm friendlier than my cousin,
But she's kinder than me.

**6** **Listen and choose the words.**

I'm **more artistic/more hardworking** than my brother,
He's **funnier/sportier** than me.
And I'm **more hardworking/more talkative** than my brother,
But he's **smarter/kinder** than me.

**7**   **Make questions. Then ask a friend.**

| | | |
|---|---|---|
| Are you | more talkative | than your sister? |
| Is your brother | friendlier | than you? |
| Is your sister | more hardworking | than your brother? |
| Is your cousin | smarter | than your cousin? |
| Is your friend | more artistic | than your friend? |

Are you friendlier than your sister?

Yes, I am!

**8** **Go to page 102. Listen and repeat the chant.**

→ Workbook page 13      Grammar      Grammar fun!    17

**What are they talking about? Listen and choose.**
a friends  b height  c age

 **Listen again and practice.**

**Teacher:** Who's taller, Carla – you or Emma?
**Emma:** I am!
**Carla:** Hmm. Let's see … I am!
**Teacher:** Wow! You're taller than Emma now!
**Emma:** But I'm still older than you, Carla!
**Teacher:** And who's smarter?
**Carla:** Oh, I don't know. We're both smart!

**11** **Read about Emma and Alex. Then ask and answer.**

**Focus**

Who's older,
you or your brother?
My brother is.

**Name:** Emma
**Born:** June 2nd, 2005
**Height:** 1 m, 60 cm
**Personality:** quiet, but friendly
**Likes:** sports and homework

**Name:** Alex
**Born:** April 24th, 2006
**Height:** 1 m, 52 cm
**Personality:** loud and funny
**Likes:** art and talking to my friends

artistic   funny   hardworking   old   quiet
short   sporty   talkative   tall   young

Who is older?

Emma is!

## Say it!

**12**  **Which syllables sound the strongest? Listen and repeat.**

**pup**-py      re-**peat**      **talk**-a-tive      hard-**work**-ing

Grammar   Pronunciation      → Workbook page 14

**1**

Which city in Colombia has a flower festival?

Wow! I think we're at the flower festival.

And look at this! It's a message!

I can help you with your game! My friend Ruby knows my name. Look for me in the parade. I'm taller than both of you today.

**2**

Hmm, I think it's from Sofia. She's very smart, but she isn't taller than us.

**3**

Look, Ruby!

It's Sofia!

**4**

Hi, Sofia! Can you help us?

Of course.

We're taking a quiz.

**5**

The first question is about the flower festival.

Yes … ?

Where are we?

→ Workbook page 15

**6**

Guess!

MEDELLÍN

Of course! We're in Medellín.

**7**

We're moving again.

Come with us, Sofia.

Where to?

# Skills: *Listening and speaking*

**Let's start!** What can you see at a circus?

**14** 🎧 1.11 **What's life like in a circus family?
Listen and say the letters.**

**a**

Show time in the circus.

**b**

Sonia at home.

**c**

The circus at night.

**d**

Circus life is hard work!

**15** 🎧 1.11 **Listen again and say *true* or *false*.**

1 Sonia's twelve years old.
2 Sonia's older than her brothers and sisters.
3 Sonia's family is hardworking.
4 Sonia's grandparents are clowns.
5 Sonia doesn't go to school.

**16** 🎧 1.12 **Talk Time** **Ask about a friend's family.**

What's your cousin like?     He's/She's …

What are your parents like?     They're …

# Skills: *Reading and writing*

 **What are these children good at?**

**17**  **Read and listen.**

### Hot shots

Brad Miller and his older sister, Casey, are from the United States. Brad is eleven, and Casey is thirteen. They're both sporty, and they're both very good at playing basketball.

Brad and Casey play on basketball teams. The other players on their teams are older and taller than them, but Brad and Casey are the star players. They practice basketball every day. Someday they want to play for the Los Angeles Lakers.

### Smart artists

Abby and Bianca Watson are twins. They're twelve years old, and they're from the United Kingdom. They're very good at art, and they like painting with bright colors. The twins sell their paintings in stores and art galleries.

This painting is by Abby. It's called "Nature."

**18** **Read again and answer the questions.**

1  Where are Brad and Casey from?
2  Who is older, Brad or Casey?
3  Are Brad and Casey hardworking?
4  Are Abby and Bianca from France?
5  Is Bianca older than Abby?
6  Where do they sell their paintings?

**Your turn!**

**Think of someone you know.**
How old are they?
What are they good at?
What do they work hard at?

**Now write about it in your notebook.**

# How do
# ant families
## work
## together?

## 1 🎧 1.14 Listen and repeat.

worker ant    colony    queen ant    drone    nest

## 2 CLIL ▶ Watch the video.

## 3 🎧 1.15 Read and listen.

Ants live in families called colonies. In each colony, ants work together in groups and help one another. Most colonies of ants live in nests, and every colony has one queen ant. The queen's job is to make lots and lots of eggs for the colony.

There are also drone ants and worker ants in colonies. The drones help the queen ant to make eggs, and the worker ants do all of the other jobs. There are always lots of worker ants. Some of them make the nest and keep it neat and clean. Other worker ants find food, like leaves, and bring it back to the nest.

Guess What!

*Some ants can live for up to 30 years!*

## 4 Answer the questions.

1 What are ant families called?
2 What does the queen ant do?
3 What do the drone ants do?
4 What do the worker ants do?

## 5 What do you like about working in a group?

Let's collaborate!

OUR FAMILIES ALBUM

describe
interview
decorate
prepare
think
plan

# On the playground

Look!

Guess What!

**1** (2.01) Listen and look.

**2** (2.02) Listen and repeat. Then match.

**a** cry  **b** litter  **c** help others  **d** hop  **e** shout
**f** skip  **g** laugh  **h** text a friend  **i** throw a ball  **j** use a cell phone

**3** (2.03) Listen and say the numbers. Then practice with a friend.

They're skipping.     Number 2!

**4** (My World) What do you do in school? Ask and answer.

**5**  **Read and listen.**

# Our school rules

✓
- We should be hardworking and listen to the teachers.
- We should be polite and help people.
- We should put litter in the trash cans.

✗
- We shouldn't shout in class.
- We shouldn't be naughty or laugh at people.
- We shouldn't litter on the ground.

**6**  **Read and say *should* or *shouldn't*.**

1  We           do our homework.
2  We           eat and drink in the classroom.
3  We           use cell phones in school.
4  We           wash our hands before lunch.
5  We           listen to music in the classroom.
6  We           be quiet in the library.

**Focus!**

We **should** be polite and help people.
We **shouldn't** shout in class.

**7**  **Make school rules with a friend.**

We should play nicely with our friends.     We shouldn't run in the classroom.

**8**  **Go to page 102. Listen and repeat the chant.**

 Grammar fun!

**9** (2.06) **What does Alex have in school? Listen and choose.**

**a** a computer game **b** a cell phone **c** a pencil case

**10** (2.06) **Listen again and practice.**

| | |
|---|---|
| **Teacher:** | OK, Pedro. Read us the story, please. |
| **Alex:** | Uh-oh! |
| **Teacher:** | Alex! Do you have a cell phone? |
| **Alex:** | Yes, I do. |
| **Teacher:** | You shouldn't use cell phones in school. Bring me the phone, please. |
| **Alex:** | Here you are. I'm sorry. |
| **Teacher:** | OK, now … |
| **Pedro:** | Uh-oh! |

**Focus**

Bring me the phone, please.
Tell the class about your vacation, please.

**11** (Think) **Read and match. Then give instructions to your friend.**

**1** Give Anna your book, please.

**2** Bring me the ball, please.

**3** Tell the class about your vacation, please.

**4** Pass Max a ruler, please.

Bring me the ball, please.     Here you are.

## Say it!

**12** (2.07) (2.08) **Which words sound the strongest? Listen and repeat.**

**Give Anna** your **book**.     **Pass Max** a **ruler**.

Grammar fun!

Grammar  Pronunciation     → Workbook page 22

Value: Be kind to animals

# Skills: *Listening and speaking*

**Let's start!** What games do you like playing on your playground?

**14** (2.10) **How do you play *Queenie, Queenie*? Listen and say the letters.**

**15** (2.10) **Put the rules in order. Listen again and check.**

a You need more than two players.

b The Queenie throws the ball behind her. She doesn't look.

c The Queenie guesses who has the ball.

d One player is the Queenie. She takes the ball and turns around.

e Another player catches the ball.

**16** (2.11) **Talk Time** **Invent or describe a game.**

> You need … players.

> You should …

> One player …

> Another player …

# Skills: *Reading and writing*

 **Where are these schools?**

**17**  **Read and listen. Then match.**

**1** Kanta is from Bangladesh. Sometimes it is very rainy, and the children can't go to school. So a school boat comes to Kanta's village. The boat has a classroom and a small library with computers. Students study hard. Kanta studies for three hours every day. She learns math, reading, writing, English, and Bengali.

**a**

**2** Alfie is from the United Kingdom. He loves reading, and he often goes to the library at his school. The library is in a bus on the playground! The bus has two floors, and there are lots of books. Students can also go to the library before and after school with their parents.

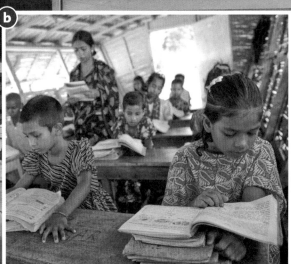
**b**

**18** **Read again and say *true*, *false*, or *don't know*.**

1 Kanta goes to school on a boat.
2 Alfie studies for three hours a day.
3 There isn't a library in Kanta's school boat.
4 Alfie loves reading.
5 There are computers in Alfie's library.
6 Kanta studies every day.

**Your turn!**
Design an unusual school.
Where is it: on a boat, in a plane, in a treehouse?
What subjects do the students study?
What rules should they follow?

**Now write about it in your notebook.**

→ Workbook page 25

# Where are
## the places
### on the map?

Central Park East Scho

Hudson River

Metropolitan Museum

N
W · E
S

Central Park Zoo

Time Warner Center

**1** 🎧 2.13 **Listen and repeat.**

**1** north

**5** compass

**4** west

**2** east

**3** south

**2** 📹 CLIL **Watch the video.**

**3** 🎧 2.14 **Read and listen.**

A compass helps us find places on a map. This map of New York Central Park shows what is in and close to the park.

To the southwest of the park, we can see a big shopping mall, and we can see a zoo in the southeast. To the west of the park, there is the Hudson River. It runs from the north to the south of New York State. In the east of the park, we can see a famous museum with art from around the world. To the northeast of the park, there's a school.

This map has a compass. It shows N, E, S, and W. It's easy to find places you want to visit.

**4** **Answer the questions.**

1 What's to the southwest of the park?
2 Where's the Hudson River on the map?
3 Where's the school on the map?
4 What do N, E, S and W mean?

**5** **When do you use a map with a compass?**

**Guess What!**
The very first maps showed the stars, not our world!

## Let's collaborate!

SIGNS FOR OUR SUSTAINABLE SCHOOL

write

match

sketch

display   tour   discuss

CLIL: Geography

# Review Units 1 and 2

**1**  **Read, listen, and choose the words.**

This is my pen pal, Lola. She's from **Brazil/Mexico**. We're both **eleven/twelve**, but she's **older/younger** than me. She was born on October **2nd/4th**, and I was born on October **22nd/24th**.

Lola and I are both **sporty/artistic**, and we love **painting/soccer**. I think she's a little **smarter/kinder** than me, though.

Lola writes to me every month, and she sends me photographs – like this one. Sometimes we **phone/text** each other. Lola is very **funny/shy**, and her letters always make me **laugh/smile**.

Lola says I **should/shouldn't** visit her one day. I'd love to!

Nadia

**2** **Read again and correct the sentences.**
1 Nadia is eleven years old.
2 Lola was born on November fourth.
3 Nadia is older than Lola.
4 Lola sends Nadia paintings.
5 Lola isn't very funny.

**3** **Think of a friend or pen pal. Ask and answer.**

Where's he/she from?
When was he/she born?
What's he/she like?

**4** **Write about your friend or pen pal in your notebook.**

34

→ Workbook page 28

# 5 Play the game.

**17** You _____ work hard in school.

**18** born? / friend / was / your / When

**19** GO BACK TWO SQUARES!

**20** GOOD JOB!

**16** GO FORWARD ONE SQUARE!

**15** A _____ person likes running, hopping, and skipping!

**14** aunt / Mexico? / from / your / Is

**13** You shouldn't _____ at other people.

**9** A _____ person talks a lot.

**10** THROW AGAIN!

**11** You shouldn't _____ cell phones in school.

**12** artistic / parents / you? / more / than / Are / your

**8** homework? / always / you / do / your / Do

**7** START AGAIN!

**6** father / the / States? / your / Is / from / United

**5** You shouldn't _____ on the playground.

**START**

**1** born / Russia? / Were / in / you

**2** A _____ person often helps other people.

**3** shyer, / you / your / Who / is / or / friend ?

**4** shyer, / you / your / Who / is / or / friend ?

**Blue** Make a question.

**Orange** Say the missing words.

# 3 Under the ocean

Look!

Guess What!

**1** (3.01) **Listen and look.**

**2** (3.02) **Listen and repeat. Then match.**

**a** crab  **b** dolphin  **c** jellyfish  **d** octopus  **e** seal
**f** shark  **g** starfish  **h** stingray  **i** turtle  **j** whale

**3** (3.03) (Think) **Listen and guess the animals. Then practice with a friend.**

It has gray fur. It's smaller than a dolphin.    It's a seal!

**4** (My World) **What's your favorite sea animal? Ask and answer.**

**5** (3.04) **Read and listen.**

Dolphins are the most intelligent sea animals. They are the friendliest, too.

Blue whales are the biggest sea animals. They are the heaviest and the strongest, too.

Great white sharks are the most dangerous sharks, but they aren't the most dangerous sea animals.

Box jellyfish are the most dangerous sea animals.

**Focus**

the strongest
the heaviest
the most dangerous

**6** **Read and say *true* or *false*.**

1 Blue whales are the weakest sea animals.

2 Dolphins are the most dangerous sea animals.

3 Great white sharks are the most dangerous sharks.

4 Box jellyfish are the friendliest sea animals.

**7** **Make sentences about sea animals. Then talk to a friend.**

Turtles are the most beautiful sea animals.

Yes, I agree.

No, I don't agree. I think dolphins are the most beautiful.

## Say it!

**8** (3.05) (3.06) **Which syllables sound the strongest? Listen and repeat.**

**Jell**yfish are **dan**gerous. **Dol**phins are in**tell**igent.

Grammar fun!

**9** (3.07) **What are they talking about? Listen and choose.**

    **a** land animals  **b** birds  **c** sea animals

**10** (3.07) **Listen again and practice.**

**Carla:** Hi, Alex. What are you doing?

**Alex:** I'm taking a quiz about animals.

**Carla:** Can I help?

**Alex:** OK. Question one. Which sea animal is the fastest? Is it a turtle, a dolphin, or a seal?

**Carla:** Hmm. I think it's a dolphin. Yes. A dolphin.

**Alex:** Yes! Good job!

**Carla:** OK. Question two …

**Focus**

Which sea animal is the fastest?
It's a dolphin.

**11** (3.08) (Think) **Look at the quiz. Make questions and ask and answer. Then listen and check.**

    Which fish is the heaviest?       It's a whale shark.

## Are you an animal whiz? Try our animal quiz.

**1 fish/heavy?**
  **a)** blue shark
  **b)** whale shark
  **c)** great white shark

**2 bird/strong?**
  **a)** eagle
  **b)** penguin
  **c)** owl

**3 land animal/strong?**
  **a)** gorilla
  **b)** elephant
  **c)** bear

**4 land animal/tall?**
  **a)** kangaroo
  **b)** panda
  **c)** giraffe

**5 sea animal/slow?**
  **a)** crab
  **b)** seahorse
  **c)** starfish

**6 land animal/dangerous?**
  **a)** hippo
  **b)** lion
  **c)** tiger

**12** (3.09) **Go to page 102. Listen and repeat the chant.**

                                 Grammar                        → Workbook page 32

## 13 🎧 3.10 Read and listen.

**1**
*What is a dolphin family called?*

What? My feet are wet!

Where are we now?

Let's see.

**2**
We're in Africa.

I think this is the Indian Ocean.

It's beautiful.

**3**
What's that? Is it trash?

I don't know.

**4**
Look! It's a baby dolphin.

Poor thing!

**5**
Quick! Help me find some shells.

Capu has the biggest shell.

**6**
Cut it like this …

Be careful, Jack!

**7**
Look! It's the dolphin's pod.

They're very friendly.

→ Workbook page 33

**8**
They're saying thank you!

It was a pleasure!

Value: Keep our seas and oceans clean

41

## Skills: *Listening and speaking*

**Let's start!** **What can you see at an aquarium?**

**14** 🎧 3.11 **Which animals do they see? Listen and say the letters.**

See our baby dolphins.

Touch a stingray.

Feed our friendly seals.

Meet Otto.

Get close to our sharks.

**15** 🎧 3.11 **Listen again and say the missing words.**
1 Otto is the _____ octopus in the world.
2 Ava and Paco see _____ baby dolphins.
3 Ava thinks _____ are dangerous.
4 The time is _____ .
5 They can feed the _____ at a quarter after three.

**16** 🎧 3.12 **Talk Time** **Plan a trip for this weekend.**

Where would you like to go this weekend?

I'd like to go to …

How can you get there?

You can go by …

## Skills: *Reading and writing*

 **What does the Sea Turtle Rescue Center do?**

**17**  **Read and listen.**

# Save Our Sea Turtles

Turtles are one of the most beautiful animals in the ocean, but they are also in danger. How can we help them?

We should keep our oceans clean. Turtles eat jellyfish, crabs, other sea animals, and plants. Dirty oceans are dangerous to turtles and the food they eat.

We should protect turtle nests. Turtles lay their eggs in nests on the beach. Sometimes birds and other animals eat the eggs or baby turtles.

# Sea Turtle Rescue Center

The Sea Turtle Rescue Center has safe beaches for turtles and their nests. It helps sick turtles in its animal hospital. Then it puts the healthy turtles back into the ocean. Turtles are happiest in the ocean.

**18** **Read again and answer the questions.**

1 Are turtles dangerous?
2 How can we help turtles?
3 What do turtles eat?
4 Where do turtles lay their eggs?
5 What does the Sea Turtle Rescue Center do?
6 Where are turtles happiest?

 **Your turn!**

**Think of a sea animal.**
Where does it live?
What does it eat?
Is it in danger?

Now write about it in your notebook.

# What is an **underwater food chain?**

## 1 🎧 3.14 Listen and repeat.

**1** sunlight  **2** producer  **3** primary consumer  **4** secondary consumer

## 2 CLIL ▶ Watch the video.

## 3 🎧 3.15 Read and listen.

Many plants and animals live underwater. How does an underwater food chain work? It needs sunlight, producers, primary consumers, and secondary consumers.

Sunlight shines on the ocean, and some sunlight goes under the water. Plants use the sunlight to make, or produce, food inside their leaves. We call these plants "producers."

Fish and other sea animals can't make their own food. They need to eat, or consume, plants and other fish. Some small sea animals or fish eat underwater plants. We call these fish "primary consumers."

Then bigger sea animals or fish, like stingray, eat smaller fish and other sea animals. They are called "secondary consumers." Big secondary consumers like sharks eat animals like seals!

**Guess What!**
Great white sharks can live for up to three months without food.

## 4 Answer the questions.

1 What helps plants to make food inside their leaves?
2 Are producers plants or animals?
3 What do we call fish that eat plants?
4 What do secondary consumers eat?

## 5 Which other food chains can you describe?

**Let's collaborate!**

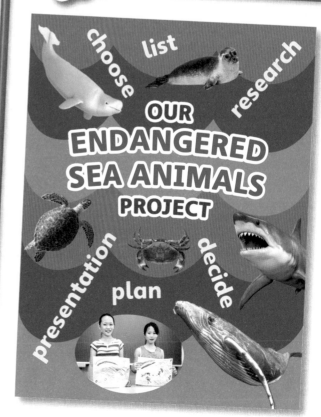

choose · list · research · OUR ENDANGERED SEA ANIMALS PROJECT · presentation · plan · decide

→ Workbook page 36    CLIL: Science

# 4 Gadgets

Look!
▶

Guess What!

**1** 🎧 4.01 **Listen and look.**

**2** 🎧 4.02 **Listen and repeat. Then match.**

**a** digital camera    **b** e-reader    **c** games console    **d** headphones    **e** laptop
**f** MP4 player    **g** smartphone    **h** tablet    **i** television    **j** video camera

**3** 🎧 4.03 *Think!* **Listen and answer the questions. Then practice with a friend.**

Can you listen to music on an MP4 player?    Yes, you can!

**4** *My World* **What gadgets do you have? Ask and answer.**

## Our class visit to Technology Live

**5**  **Read and listen.**

Luisa: I listened to music on an MP4 player in a watch!

Tia: I didn't play games or watch a movie. I studied English on an e-reader.

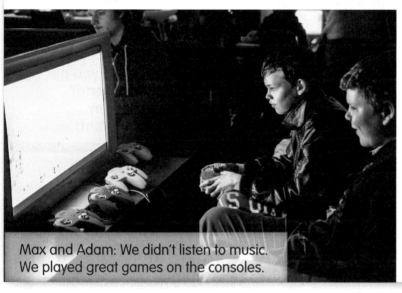

Max and Adam: We didn't listen to music. We played great games on the consoles.

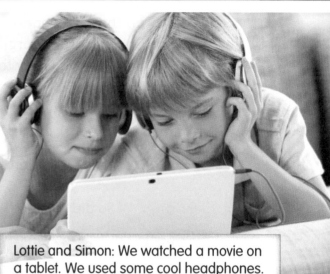

Lottie and Simon: We watched a movie on a tablet. We used some cool headphones.

**6** **Read and say the names.**

1 They played on the games consoles.
2 She didn't watch a movie.
3 She used an e-reader.
4 She listened to music on an MP4 player.
5 They didn't play on the games consoles. They watched a movie.

**Focus**

I **studied** English.
I **listened** to music on an MP4 player.
We **didn't listen** to music.

**7** **My World** **Make true and false sentences about you. Then talk to a friend.**

| | | |
|---|---|---|
| listened to | a games console | yesterday evening |
| watched | my MP4 player | last night |
| played on | television | last Saturday |
| used | my laptop | this morning before school |

I watched television this morning before school.    False.

**8**  **Go to page 102. Listen and repeat the chant.**

**9** (4.06) **Who did Emma visit last weekend? Listen and choose.**

a her cousins   b her friends   c her grandparents

**10** (4.06) **Listen again and practice.**

**Carla:** Hi, Emma. What did you do last weekend?
**Emma:** I visited my grandparents.
**Carla:** Was it fun?
**Emma:** Yes, it was great.
**Carla:** What did you do?
**Emma:** We watched television, and we played
on their new games console.
**Carla:** Do your grandparents have a games console?
**Emma:** Yes, they do. They love playing games!

**11** (My World) **Choose four activities you did last weekend.
Then talk to some friends.**

What did you do last weekend?          I played soccer.

So did I.          I didn't. I visited my cousins.

### Focus

What did you do
last weekend?
I visited my
grandparents.

listened to
music

played with
friends

played
soccer

called a
friend

used a
laptop

played on a
games console

cleaned my
room

painted a
picture

helped my
parents

walked in
the park

studied
English

watched
television

## Say it!

**12** (4.07) (4.08) **Can you hear the different endings? Listen and repeat.**

/d/                  /t/                  /id/
played          watched          visited

Grammar   Pronunciation          → Workbook page 40

# 13 🎧 4.09 **Read and listen.**

**1** It's cold.

Do trees grow in Antarctica?

There's nothing here!

Only snow! Let's go in that hut.

**2** I think we're in Antarctica.

It's 1950. Look at this diary.

**3** Listen to this!

...rrived this ...ning. The hut ...ery cold, and ... don't have any ...ood.

**4** Where are they now?

What is it, Capu?

**5** Over there!

We should help them!

**6** Let's use these blankets.

I'll ask for help. I can use the tablet.

**7**

**8** Thanks for helping us!

It's thanks to our tablet!

Yes, what a wonderful gadget!

→ Workbook page 41

Value: Use technology wisely

# Skills: *Listening and speaking*

**Let's start!** Which gadgets do you have?

**14** (4.10) **What were the first gadgets? Listen and match.**

Adam Osborne    Martin Cooper    Ralph Baer

**a**

**b**

**c**

1973    1981    1967–1968

**15** (4.10) **Listen again and answer the questions.**

1 What was the name of the first games console?
2 How many games were there on the first games console?
3 What was the name of the first laptop?
4 How long was the first cell phone?
5 Where did Martin Cooper get the idea for a cell phone?

**16** (4.11) (Talk Time) **Decide which inventions are the most useful.**

Which invention is the most useful?    I think it's the …

What do you use it to do?    I use it to …

# Skills: *Reading and writing*

 **What does Max like using his smartphone for?**

**17**  **Read and listen.**

Max is eleven years old, and he likes making movies with his smartphone. We asked him some questions.

*How do you make movies?*
I think of a story with my friends. Then they act out the story, and I film it.

*Where do you make your movies?*
We usually go to the park and make the movie outside. Then we go home and edit the movie on my laptop. Editing means choosing the best parts of the movie. I add music and special effects on my laptop, too.

*Where do you watch your movies?*
On the laptop. Sometimes our parents watch them. They think the movies are funny.

*Is making movies difficult?*
No. It's easy with a smartphone!

**18** **Read again and correct the sentences.**
1  Max is twelve years old.
2  He likes making movies with his digital camera.
3  He makes movies with his cousins.
4  He always makes movies in the park.
5  He edits the movies on a games console.
6  His parents think the movies are boring.

**Your turn!**
Think of your favorite gadget.
What is it?
What do you like doing with it?

**Now write about it in your notebook.**

# How do we read a line chart?

**1** 🎧 4.13 **Listen and repeat.**

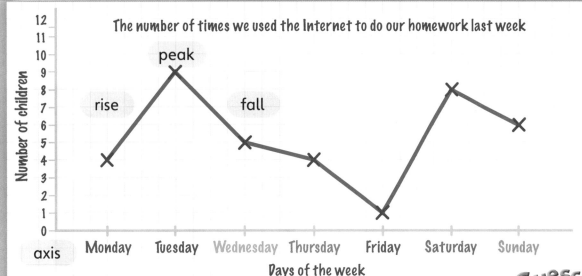

The number of times we used the Internet to do our homework last week

Number of children: 0, 1, 2, 3, 4, 5, 6, 7, 8, 9, 10, 11, 12

peak · rise · fall

axis

Monday · Tuesday · Wednesday · Thursday · Friday · Saturday · Sunday

Days of the week

| Mon | Tues | Wed | Thurs | Fri | Sat | Sun |
|---|---|---|---|---|---|---|
| ||||  ||||| | ||||| | ||||  | | | ||||| | ||||| |
| |||| | | | data | | ||| | | |

**Guess What!**
Different names for the number 0 include zero, nought, zilch, and zip.

**2** CLIL ▶ **Watch the video.**

**3** 🎧 4.14 **Look at activity 1. Listen and read the data on the line chart.**

**4** **Answer the questions.**

1 How many children used the Internet to do their homework on Wednesday?
2 When was there a big rise in the number of children using the Internet?
3 When was there a bigger fall – between Tuesday and Wednesday or between Thursday and Friday?
4 Which day shows the peak number of children using the Internet?

**5** **What different data can you put in a line chart?**

**Let's collaborate!**

OUR SCREEN TIME SURVEY

list · ask · record · recommend · conclude · bar chart

# Review Units 3 and 4

**1** (4.15) **Read, listen, and choose the words.**

On my eleventh birthday, I **visit/visited** my favorite **art gallery/movie theater** in London with my family. The movie theater has the **biggest/smallest** screen in the United Kingdom, and it was great.

We watched a very **dangerous/interesting** movie. It was called *Under the Ocean*.

The movie was in 3-D, and we **need/needed** special **headphones/glasses**.

There were lots of beautiful sea animals and some funny ones, too. The **strongest/funniest** one was a crab with a jellyfish on its head! The most **exciting/dangerous** animals were the sea snakes.

We also **listened/learned** about taking care of our oceans.

We should keep them **clean/dirty**.

It was my favorite birthday ever!

Tom

**2** **Read again and answer the questions.**

1 How old was Tom?
2 Where did he visit on his birthday?
3 What movie did he watch?
4 What was the funniest sea animal?
5 What did Tom learn about oceans?

**3** (My World) **Think of a visit to the movie theater. Ask and answer.**

What movie did you watch?
Was it in 3-D?
What was it about?

**4** **Write about a movie theater visit in your notebook.**

56

→ Workbook page 46

**5** Play the game.

**TECHNOLOGY FAIR**

**1** Start

**2** Which is the strongest land animal?

**3** Watch television/ last night

**4** Free headphones! Miss a turn!

**5** Use an e-reader/ before school

Which sea animal has eight legs?

**7** Visit grandparents/ last weekend

**6** Which is the most dangerous sea animal?

Play on the games consoles! Miss a turn!

Which is the most intelligent sea animal?

**11** Play on a laptop/ yesterday afternoon

**12** You lose your smartphone. Go back to the start.

**13** Listen to music/ yesterday evening

**14** Which dangerous sea animal has a lot of teeth?

**18** Finish!

**17** Study English/ last Saturday

**16** Which is the tallest land animal?

**15** Watch the digital jellyfish. Miss a turn!

**Green**
Answer the questions.

**Purple**
Make true sentences using these words.

57

# The natural world

**Look!**
▶

Guess What!

**1** (5.01) **Listen and look.**

**2** (5.02) **Listen and repeat. Then match.**

**a** cave   **b** desert   **c** forest   **d** island   **e** jungle
**f** lake   **g** mountain   **h** river   **i** volcano   **j** waterfall

**3** (5.03) (Think) **Listen and say *true* or *false*. Then practice with a friend.**

You can climb a mountain.     True!

**4** (My World) **Which of these things would you like to see? Ask and answer.**

**5** 🎧 5.04 **Read and listen.**

My family went to Iceland. It was very beautiful.
We saw mountains and high waterfalls.

We had lunch on a volcano! We drank
hot chocolate with our lunch.

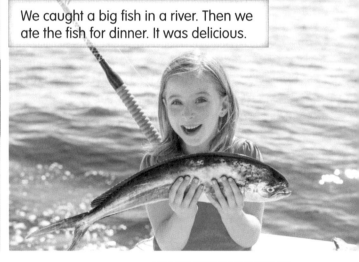

We caught a big fish in a river. Then we
ate the fish for dinner. It was delicious.

We swam in a lake. The water was warm.

**6** (Think) **Read and correct the sentences.**

1 The family went to Russia.
2 They had lunch in a café.
3 They drank orange juice.
4 They swam in a river.
5 They caught a seal in a river.
6 They ate an octopus for dinner.

**Focus**

have – had
go – went
see – saw
swim – swam
eat – ate
drink – drank
catch – caught

**7** (My World) **Think about your vacation last summer. Then ask and answer.**

Where did you go on vacation last summer?
What did you do?
What did you see?
What did you eat and drink?

I went to Baha in Mexico. We
swam in the ocean, and we saw
whales. We didn't see any sharks.

# Say it!

**8** 🎧 5.05 🎧 5.06 **Which words sound the strongest? Listen and repeat.**

We **didn't go** to a **mountain**.     We **went** to a **lake**.

→ Workbook page 49          Grammar   Pronunciation          Grammar fun! ▶          61

**9** 🔊 5.07 **Where did Emma go on vacation? Listen and choose.**

**a** a desert **b** a jungle **c** an island

**10** 🔊 5.07 **Listen again and practice.**

**Alex:** Hi, Emma. What are you doing?

**Emma:** I'm making an album about my vacation. Look, I went to Easter Island.

**Alex:** Cool! Did you see these statues?

**Emma:** Yes, I did. They were amazing.

**Alex:** Did you climb the statues?

**Emma:** No, I didn't! You shouldn't climb on statues, Alex.

**Alex:** I know. It was a joke!

**Focus**

Did you see statues?
Yes, I did.
No, I didn't.

**11** Think **Think about Alex's vacation scrapbook. Then ask and answer.**

| see animals | swim in a lake | climb a mountain | have a picnic | drink coffee |
| go on a boat trip | see a cave | catch a fish | take photographs | visit a museum |

Did he see animals?        Yes, he did.

Did he swim in a lake?        No, he didn't.

the mountain we climbed

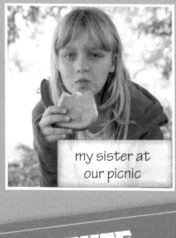

my sister at our picnic

WHITE SHARK *boat trip*

penguins at the beach

my grandpa and grandma at the market

**12** 🔊 5.08 **Go to page 103. Listen and repeat the chant.**

Grammar fun!

62

Grammar

→ Workbook page 50

**13** 🎧 5.09  **Read and listen.**

**1**

Which country is Hollywood in?

Help! I can't see anything. I don't like the dark!

Don't worry, Ruby. We can use the tablet.

**2**

We're in a cave.

How do we get out?

Let's try this path.

**3**

Oh, no! I don't like bats!

Don't worry, Sofia.

Let's try the other path.

**4**

Wow!

Cut!

**5**

Oh, dear!

We're very sorry!

SCRIPT

Don't worry! You can help us.

**6**

Four actors didn't come this morning.

HOLLYWOOD

We're in Hollywood, in the United States!

**7**

Oh, no! I'm not good at acting.

You're a great actor, Jack!

Action!

→ Workbook page 51

**8**

That was great!

And cut! Thank you, everyone.

Value: Encourage your friends

63

# Skills: *Listening and speaking*

 **Let's start!** | **What is the most interesting animal you can think of?**

**14** 🎧 5.10 **Where can you find them? Listen and say *rain forest* or *desert*.**

bilby

armadillo lizard

rafflesia

parrot flower

baseball plant

**15** 🎧 5.10 **Listen again and choose the words.**

1 Bilbys have long **ears/legs**.
2 Armadillo lizards are **big/small**.
3 The rafflesia is the **oldest/biggest** flower in the world.
4 The parrot flower looks like a **bird/bat**.
5 The baseball plant grows in the **United States/China**.

**16** 🎧 5.11 (Talk Time) **Identify animals and plants.**

What's this animal called?     It's called a …

What's this plant called?     It's called a …

# Skills: *Reading and writing*

**Look below!** What did Billy do on vacation?

**17** 🎧 5.12 **Read and listen.**

### My vacation in the Volcanoes National Park.

We arrived yesterday. The park is very beautiful. There are mountains, volcanoes, and rain forests. There are also about 480 mountain gorillas in the park. We wanted to see them.

You can only visit the gorillas with a guide. We got up very early this morning and walked through the forest for three hours. Then our guide pointed in front of us. We saw a gorilla family!

There was a mother gorilla with a baby and a father gorilla. Father gorillas are called silverbacks, and they're very strong. The gorillas didn't hide – they watched us, too! We stayed close to them for one hour. Then we went back to our hotel. It was the most exciting day of my life!

**18** **Read again and answer the questions.**
1 Did Billy go to a desert?
2 How many gorillas live in the park?
3 Did Billy visit the gorillas at night?
4 What are father gorillas called?
5 Were the gorillas interested in Billy?
6 Did he enjoy meeting the gorillas?

**Your turn!** Think of your favorite vacation.
Where did you go?
What did you do?
What did you see?

**Now write about it in your notebook.**

→ Workbook page 53

# What happens when a
# volcano
## erupts?

# 1 🎧 5.13 Listen and repeat.

1 vent  2 crater  3 lava  4 rock  5 ash

# 2 CLIL ▶ Watch the video.

# 3 🎧 5.14 Read and listen.

Volcanoes look like mountains, but volcanoes have a vent inside and a crater at the top. Sometimes they erupt, and very hot, red material comes up the volcano's vent and runs into the crater. This hot material is called lava, and it is very dangerous.

Next, ash and rocks fly high into the air, and the lava runs down the sides of the volcano. After the eruption, the lava gets colder, and it turns to rock.

Lava sometimes runs over plants, and then they stop growing.

A volcano that erupts is called an active volcano. There are about 1,500 active volcanoes in the world.

**Guess What!**

The world's largest active volcano is Mauna Loa in Hawaii. It is 4,169 m tall.

# 4 Answer the questions.

1  What does a volcano look like?
2  What is at the top of the volcano?
3  What happens to the very hot, red material when a volcano erupts?
4  How many active volcanoes are there?

# 5 Which volcano would you like to see?

**Let's collaborate!**

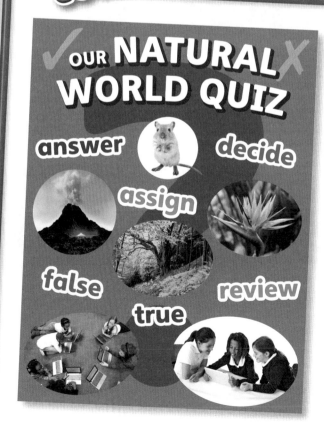

OUR NATURAL WORLD QUIZ

answer   decide   assign   false   review   true

Look!

Guess What!

**1** 🎧 6.01 **Listen and look.**

**2** 🎧 6.02 **Listen and repeat. Then match.**

a clean the bathroom     b cook dinner     c dry the dishes     d set the table
e make my bed     f take the trash out     g sweep the floor
h clean my bedroom     i wash my clothes     j water the plants

**3** 🎧 6.03 (Think) **Listen and guess the answers. Then practice with a friend.**

What's he doing?     Hmm ... he's taking the trash out!

**4** (My World) **How often do you help at home? Ask and answer.**

**5** (6.04) **Read and listen. Then read and say the names.**

○ TUESDAY

○ Ellen – please clean your room and set the table.

○ Alfie – please make your bed and water the plants.

○ Max – please take the trash out and sweep the floor.

○ Thanks, Mom

**1** I have to water the plants, and I have to make my bed. I don't have to take the trash out.

**2** My sister has to clean her room, and she has to set the table. She doesn't have to make her bed.

**3** My brother doesn't have to clean his room. He has to sweep the floor, and he has to take the trash out.

**Focus**

I have to make my bed.
I don't have to take the trash out.

**6** **Read and answer the questions.**

1 Does Ellen have to make her bed?
2 Does Max have to clean his room?
3 Does Alfie have to take the trash out?
4 Does Ellen have to set the table?
5 Does Max have to sweep the floor?

**7** (Think) **Write an instruction for a friend. Then mime and guess.**

Please clean the bathroom.    Do you have to clean the bathroom?    Yes, I do.

# Say it!

**8** (6.05) (6.06) **Can you hear the different endings? Listen and repeat.**

| /s/ | /z/ | /iz/ |
|-----|-----|------|
| plants | clothes | dishes |

Grammar fun!

71

**9**  **What does Pedro like doing? Listen and choose.**

a collecting the books    b watering the plants
c feeding the fish

**10**  **Listen again and practice.**

**Alex:** What do you have to do today, Pedro?
**Pedro:** I have to collect the books. What about you?
**Alex:** I have to water the plants.
**Pedro:** Who has to feed the fish today?
**Alex:** Emma does.
**Pedro:** Lucky her – I love feeding the fish.
        Who has to feed the fish tomorrow?
**Alex:** You do.
**Pedro:** Oh, good!

**Focus**

What do you have to do?
I have to collect the books.
Who has to feed the fish?
Luisa does.

**11**  **Look at the classroom schedule.
Then ask and answer.**

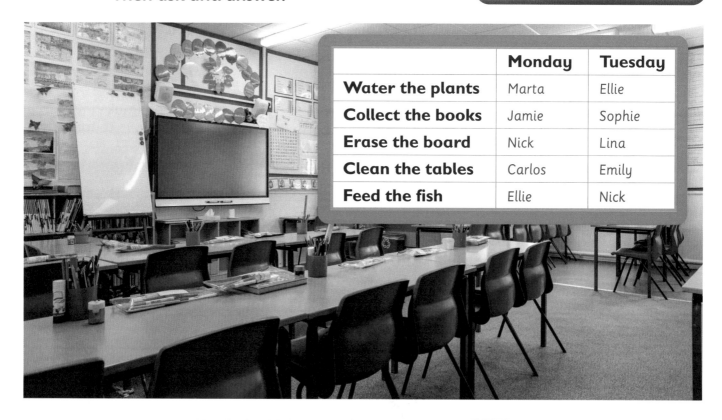

|  | Monday | Tuesday |
|---|---|---|
| **Water the plants** | Marta | Ellie |
| **Collect the books** | Jamie | Sophie |
| **Erase the board** | Nick | Lina |
| **Clean the tables** | Carlos | Emily |
| **Feed the fish** | Ellie | Nick |

Who has to erase the board on Monday?     Nick!

What does Nick have to do on Tuesday?     He has to feed the fish.

**12**  **Go to page 103. Listen and repeat the chant.**

              Grammar             → Workbook page 58

🎧 6.09 **Read and listen.**

1

Which river flows through Egypt?

It's a palace in ancient Egypt!

This must be the River Nile.

2

What's wrong?

The king wants to visit today. We have to finish the palace!

We can help.

3

4

Thank you for your help!

It's beautiful!

5

Look! The King is coming.

6

Oh, no! Where's the key to the palace?

7

Capu! Stop!

No, it's OK. He's a smart monkey!

8

Welcome, King!

It was the key!

Good job, Capu!

→ Workbook page 59

Value: Help other people

73

# Skills: *Listening and speaking*

**Let's start!** What does your home look like?

**14** 🎧 6.10 **Where do these families live? Listen and say the letters.**

**a**

**b**

**c**

**d**

**15** 🎧 6.10 **Listen again and say *true* or *false*.**

1 The transparent house is in Japan.
2 The cave house doesn't have a bathroom.
3 The family with the houseboat lives in the United Kingdom.
4 Six giraffes live at the Giraffe Manor hotel.

**16** 🎧 6.11 **Talk Time** **Design your own home.**

> It's a cave house. It has ...

> There are ... bedrooms.

> The living room is ...

> The garden has ...

# Skills: *Reading and writing*

 **Look below!** **What does Sasha do to help at home?**

**17**  **Read and listen.**

*Sasha Rudd lives on a farm.*
*What does she have to do at home?*

I get up at six o'clock in the morning, and I help with the animals. We have cows, goats, and hens on our farm.

I feed the hens every morning before school. I have to collect the eggs, too. This morning I found six eggs. We had them for breakfast.

On the weekend, I help with the goats. I have to feed them, and I milk them, too. We make cheese with the milk.

I don't have to help with the cows much, but sometimes I have to clean the cowshed after school. That isn't my favorite job!

Life on a farm is hard work, but it's fun. Come and stay!

**18** **Read again and say the missing words.**

1 Sasha ▇▇▇▇ ▇▇▇▇ at six o'clock in the morning.
2 There are cows, ▇▇▇▇ , and goats on Sasha's farm.
3 Sasha had eggs for ▇▇▇▇ this morning.
4 Sasha helps with the ▇▇▇▇ on the weekend.
5 Sasha's family makes ▇▇▇▇ with goat's milk.
6 Sasha has to ▇▇▇▇ the cowshed after school.

**Your turn!**

**Think about your day.**
What do you do before and after school?
Do you have to help at home or school?

**Now write about it in your notebook.**

# What were
## castle homes
like?

## 1 🎧 6.13 Listen and repeat.

**1** tower

**2** candle

**3** fire

**4** wall

## 2 🎬 Watch the video.

## 3 🎧 6.14 Read and listen.

In the past, some people lived in castles. Most castles had water and big walls around them. The castle walls had tall towers in them. People climbed the towers to see things far away.

Inside the castle there was one very big hall. In this room, families had meals around a long wooden table and talked and listened to music.

Castles had very big kitchens, and people cooked food on open fires. People ate a lot of meat and also bread, fruits, and vegetables. Castles had big gardens, and people grew their own fruits and vegetables. It was very dark at night, and there were no lights. People used candles to see in the dark.

## 4 Answer the questions.

1. Where did families eat, talk, and listen to music?
2. How did people cook their food?
3. What did people grow in the garden?
4. How did people see in the dark?

## 5 Would you like to live in an old castle?

**Guess What!**
People used wood, not stone, to make the very first castles.

**Let's collaborate!**

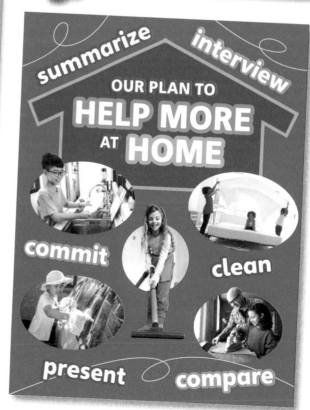
summarize  interview
OUR PLAN TO **HELP MORE** AT **HOME**
commit  clean
present  compare

# Review Units 5 and 6

 **1** 🎧 6.15 **Read, listen, and choose the words.**

**To:**

Last month, I went to Loch Ness with my youth club. Loch Ness is a big **island/lake** in **Russia/Scotland**. Some people think a **monster/whale** lives in it. It was an exciting weekend. Some of my friends swam in the lake, but I didn't. The water was very **hot/cold**. We all went on a boat trip, and we looked for the **whale/monster**, but we **saw/didn't see** it.

In the evening, we **went for a walk/ had a picnic** in the **mountains/forest** close to the lake.

Our teacher caught a **fish/monster**, and I had to help cook it for **lunch/ dinner**. Then my friend had to **dry/ wash** the dishes, but we didn't have to set **the table/the bathroom**. We didn't have one!

Becky

**2** **Read again and say** *true* **or** *false*.
1. Becky went to a lake.
2. Becky swam in the lake.
3. Becky didn't see the Loch Ness monster.
4. Becky had to help cook dinner.
5. Her friend had to dry the dishes.

**3** (My World) **Think of an exciting trip. Ask and answer.**

Where did you go?
What did you do?
What did you see?

**4** **Write about your trip in your notebook.**

→ Workbook page 64

# 5 Play the game.

**7** A _____ is a tropical forest.

**7** You don't like spiders! Miss a turn.

**6** family? / has / Who / cook / to / dinner / your / in

**8** vacation? / volcano / Did / climb / on / a / you

**6** today? / Who / clean / to / has / classroom / the

**8** sweep / before / Did / school? / you / floor / the

**9** An _____ is land with water around it.

**5** You have to _____ a messy bedroom.

**5** You don't like bats! Miss a turn.

**9** You have to _____ plants sometimes.

**4** chocolate / Did / drink / hot / you / night? / last

**4** eat / octopus / Did / breakfast? / for / you

Good job!

FINISH

**3** You have to _____ your bed in the morning.

**3** A _____ is a place under the ground.

**2** clean / bathroom? / you / have / Do / to / the

ENTER HERE

**2** trash? / Do / out / have / you / take / to / the

**1** You have to _____ dirty clothes.

**1** A _____ flows from a mountain to the ocean.

Find the hidden treasure!

**Green**
Say the missing words.

**Purple**
Make a question.

# 7 Feelings

Look!

Guess What!

**1** (7.01) **Listen and look.**

**2** (7.02) **Listen and repeat. Then match.**

**a** angry   **b** bored   **c** excited   **d** hungry   **e** interested
**f** scared   **g** surprised   **h** thirsty   **i** tired   **j** worried

**3** (7.03) **Listen and say *true* or *false*. Then practice with a friend.**

Look at picture ten. She's scared.        False!

**4** (My World) **Mime a feeling. Ask and answer.**

**5** (7.04) **Read, listen, and find. Then say the names.**

**Focus**

He's scared **because** he doesn't like spiders.

Jim

Ben          Ali

Emily     Daisy          Lucy

1 He's scared because he doesn't like spiders.
3 They're smiling because they're happy.
5 He's laughing because it's funny.

2 She's eating because she's hungry.
4 He's surprised because there's a spider.

**6**  **Read and match.**

1 Lucy is happy because …
2 Ben is suprised because …
3 Emily is hungry because …
4 Ali is scared because …
5 It's funny because …

a there's a bird on Jim's head.
b the spider is on his bananas.
c it's breakfast time.
d he really doesn't like spiders.
e she's talking to her friend.

**7** (My World) **Make sentences with a friend.**

I'm hungry because …     I'm happy because …

# Say it!

**8** (7.05) (7.06) **Does the end of the sentence go up or down? Listen and repeat.**

I'm surprised because this lesson is easy.     He's laughing because it's funny.

Grammar fun!

**Who's scared of sharks? Listen and choose.**

   **a** Emma   **b** Emma's sister   **c** Pedro

 **Listen again and practice.**

**Pedro:** Hi, Emma. How are you today?

**Emma:** I'm OK, but I'm a little tired.

**Pedro:** Why are you tired?

**Emma:** I'm tired because it was my sister's birthday yesterday. We stayed up late and watched a movie.

**Pedro:** That sounds like fun.

**Emma:** Yes, but then my sister didn't want to go to bed because she was scared.

**Pedro:** Why was she scared?

**Emma:** Because it was a movie about sharks. She's scared of sharks.

**Pedro:** Oh, no!

> **Focus**
>
> **Why** is she tired?
> She's tired **because** she stayed up late.

  **Read and match. Then ask how your friends are feeling and why.**

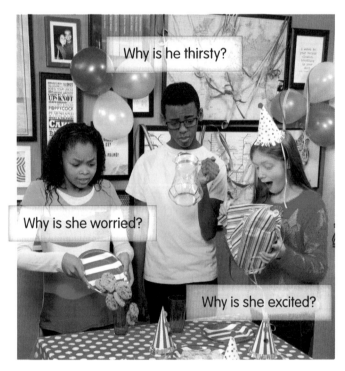

Why is he thirsty?

Why is she worried?

Why is she excited?

Why is he bored?   Why is she interested?

**a** Because there isn't any juice.   **b** Because he doesn't like reading.
**c** Because it's her birthday.   **d** Because she's reading a good book.
**e** Because the cookies aren't on the plate.

 **Go to page 103. Listen and repeat the chant.**

Grammar fun!

Grammar

→ Workbook page 68

**13** 🎧 7.09 **Read and listen.**

1

Where does the annatto plant grow?

We're in the rain forest in South America.

Why is Capu so excited?

Because this is his home!

2

Let's follow Capu!

Ow!

What's the matter, Jack?

3

It was a snake!

Don't be scared.

We'll help.

4

We need the annatto plant. It grows here.

ANNATTO PLANT

Can you show us, Capu?

5

Can you help us?

Of course. What's the matter?

6

Thank you!

→ Workbook page 69

7

Are you OK, Jack?

Yes! They made a medicine with the plant.

8

Goodbye, Capu!

We'll miss you!

Value: Respect nature

85

# Skills: *Listening and speaking*

**Let's start!** What is your favorite book and why?

**14** 🎧 7.10 What are their favorite books? Listen and match.

**a** Goodnight, Mr. Tom, Michelle Magorian

**b** Horrid Henry, Francesca Simon

Ben  Amber  George  Zoe

**c** Charlie and the Chocolate Factory, Roald Dahl

**d** Stay Out of the Basement, R.L. Stine

**15** 🎧 7.10 Listen again and choose the words.
1  "Stay Out of the Basement" is about two children and their **mother/father/uncle**.
2  The "Horrid Henry" stories are **exciting/funny/sad**.
3  **Four/Five/Six** children visit the factory in "Charlie and the Chocolate Factory."
4  "Goodnight, Mr. Tom" is about a boy and an old **man/woman/horse**.

**16** 🎧 7.11 **Talk Time** Discuss your favorite author.

Who's your favorite author?

My favorite author is …

What kind of stories does he/she write?

He/She writes …

→ Workbook page 70

## Skills: *Reading and writing*

Look below! **What is Jack climbing?**

**17** 🎧 7.12 **Read and listen.**

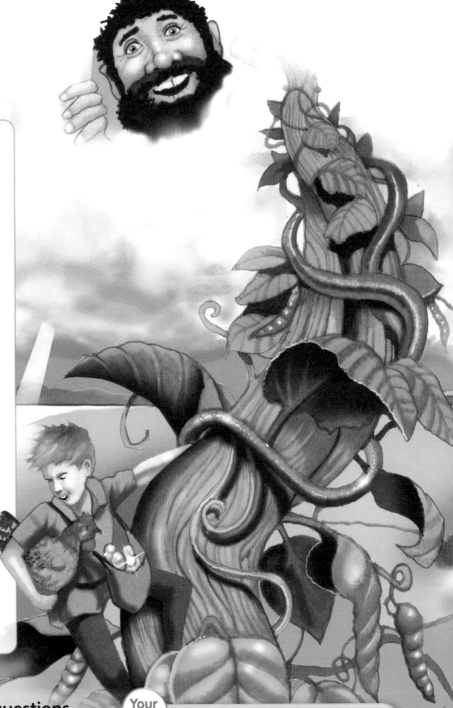

# Jack and the Beanstalk

Jack and his mother lived in a village. His mother was often worried because they didn't have any money. One day, Jack had to go to the market and sell their cow. Then he had to buy some food, but Jack only bought five beans.

Jack's mother was very angry. She threw the beans out the window. That night, they grew into a magic beanstalk. Jack and his mother were very surprised.

Jack climbed up the beanstalk. A giant lived in a castle at the top. Jack was scared, but the giant was friendly. He gave Jack a magic hen for his mother. The hen made gold eggs. Jack's mother was very happy, and Jack and the giant were friends.

**18** **Read again and answer the questions.**

1 Why was Jack's mother often worried?
2 Where did Jack have to sell the cow?
3 How many beans did Jack buy?
4 Who lived at the top of the beanstalk?
5 Why was the hen magic?
6 How did his mother feel at the end of the story?

**Your turn!**

**Think of a story you know.**
Who is in the story?
What happens in the story?
Is the story funny, exciting, sad, or scary?

**Now write about it in your notebook.**

→ Workbook page 71

# How do animals communicate?

**1** 🎧 7.13 **Listen and repeat.**

①
growl

②
flap

③
hiss

④
purr

⑤
change color

**2** 📹 CLIL **Watch the video.**

**3** 🎧 7.14 **Read and listen.**

Different animals communicate in different ways. Many animals use sounds to communicate with each other. Birds sing, lions, and tigers growl, and turtles can hiss. Chimpanzees touch hands to say "hello!" Some animals, like frogs and spiders, change color to send messages to each other.

Animals communicate how they feel with their bodies, heads, mouths, and ears. Animals show they are happy in different ways. Polar bears move their heads from side to side, some wild cats purr, and excited elephants flap their ears.

Animals show they are angry in different ways, too. Elephants move very fast, bears growl, and snakes and crocodiles hiss.

**Guess What!**
Whales jump out of the water to send messages to other whales.

**4** **Answer the questions.**

1 How do chimpanzees say "hello"?
2 How do some frogs and spiders send messages to each other?
3 What body parts do animals use to communicate?
4 How do snakes and crocodiles show they're angry?

**5** **How do you communicate your feelings to your family?**

**Let's collaborate!**

OUR **FEELINGS** COLLAGE
organize
describe
gather
ask and answer
excited
events

→ Workbook page 72

CLIL: Science

# Outdoor sports

Look!

Guess What!

**1** 🎧 8.01 **Listen and look.**

**2** 🎧 8.02 **Listen and repeat. Then match.**

**a** bodyboarding  **b** canoeing  **c** go-carting  **d** hiking  **e** rock climbing
**f** rowing  **g** scuba diving  **h** snorkeling  **i** trampolining  **j** windsurfing

**3** 🎧 8.03 **Listen and answer the questions. Then practice with a friend.**

Look at picture 5. Are they canoeing?

No, they aren't!

**4** (My World) **What activities would you like to do? Ask and answer.**

→ Workbook page 74

**5** 8.04 **Read and listen.**

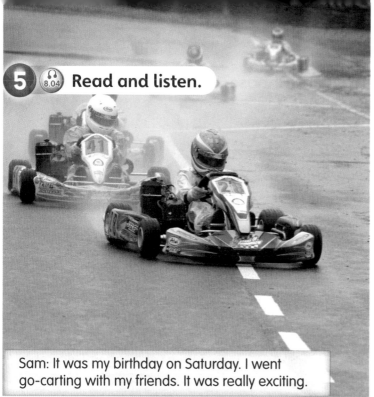

Sam: It was my birthday on Saturday. I went go-carting with my friends. It was really exciting.

Sally: I went to the country with my family. We didn't go hiking. We went canoeing!

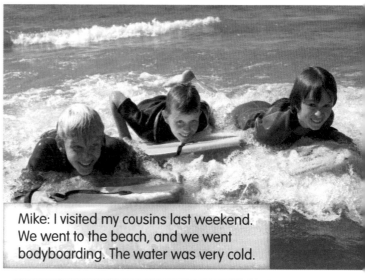

Mike: I visited my cousins last weekend. We went to the beach, and we went bodyboarding. The water was very cold.

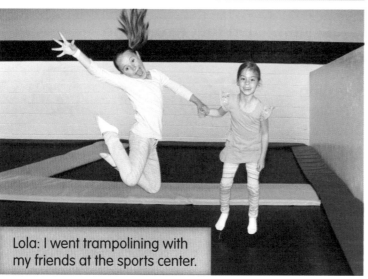

Lola: I went trampolining with my friends at the sports center.

**Focus**

They **didn't go go-carting** on Saturday.
What **did** she **do** last weekend?
She **went canoeing**.

**6** **Match the questions and answers.**

1 What did Sam do on Saturday?
2 Did Sally go hiking?
3 Did Lola go trampolining?
4 What did Mike do?

a He went bodyboarding.
b Yes, she did.
c He went go-carting.
d No, she didn't.

**7** My World **Ask and answer.**

What did you do last weekend?     I went hiking.

Did you go windsurfing?     No, I didn't. I went swimming.

**8** 8.05 **Go to page 103. Listen and repeat the chant.**

→ Workbook page 75       Grammar       Grammar fun!     93

**9** **What are they talking about? Listen and choose.**

a the weekend   b last month   c last year

 **10** **Listen again and practice.**

**Pedro:** Can I see your photographs, Carla?
**Carla:** Yes, of course – it's an album of my year.
**Pedro:** I like this photograph! Did you go windsurfing last year?
**Carla:** Yes, I did. I went on an activity vacation with my school.
**Pedro:** Great! When did you go?
**Carla:** In March. We went rowing, too.
**Pedro:** Cool! And when did you go skiing?
**Carla:** In December.
**Pedro:** Wow!

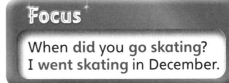

**Focus**

When **did** you **go** skating?
I **went** skating in December.

**11** **Choose four activities you did last year. Then talk to a friend.**

snorkeling      rowing       bodyboarding

sailing      canoeing      swimming      rock climbing

trampolining      windsurfing      ice-skating

fishing      go-carting      hiking      biking

Did you go skiing last year?       Yes, I did.

So did I. When did you go (skiing)?       In February.

Oh! I went in March.

## Say it!

  **12** **Does the end of the question go up or down? Listen and repeat.**

When did you go windsurfing? ↗       What did you do in March? ↗

        Grammar   Pronunciation       → Workbook page 76

**13** 🎧 8.09 **Read and listen.**

**1**

Good job, kids.
You finished the quiz.
Now off you fly,
And collect your prize.

Where can we find something to fly?

**2**

Look! There's a helicopter up there!

Yes, but how do we get there?

**3**

We can go rock climbing.

OK, but we should be safe. Put on your helmets and follow me.

**4**

Come on, kids!

Hold on tight to the ropes.

**5**

It's our town!

And there's the library!

**6**

Thanks for your help, Sofia.

Do you have to go home?

Yes, I do, but it was fun!

**7**

Goodbye, Sofia!

See you again soon!

**8**

Good job! How did you find out the answers?

It's a long story!

PRIZE

→ Workbook page 77

Value: Be safe    95

# Skills: *Listening and speaking*

 **What new hobby would you like to try?**

**14** (8.10) **Which is Malia's club? Listen and choose a picture.**

**a**

**b**

**15** (8.10) **Listen again and say *true* or *false*.**

1 Malia thinks windsurfing is boring.
2 Malia goes to a windsurfing club on Tuesdays.
3 Malia has windsurfing lessons on a lake.
4 Windsurfing can be dangerous.
5 Malia gets scared sometimes.

**16** (8.11) (Talk Time) **Plan to join a new sports club.**

What sport should we play?   Let's try …

What equipment do we need?   We need …

# Skills: *Reading and writing*

 **Look below!** **Why is this game of volleyball different?**

 **17** 8.12 **Read and listen.**

## Let's try something different!

Do you like trampolining? Try bossaball! Bossaball is like volleyball, but you play on a trampoline. There are two teams. The players hit or kick the ball over a net. The ball hits the floor, and the team gets a point.

Can you swim underwater? What about playing hockey? Underwater hockey started in the United Kingdom. Now people play it all over the world. There are two teams. The players have to push a hockey puck at the bottom of a pool. It's also called "Octopush."

Do you enjoy bodyboarding? Do you have a dog? How about a dog surfing competition? Dog surfing competitions are popular in California, in the United States. There are competitions every year.

**18** **Read again and say the missing words.**

1 Bossaball is like _____ .
2 You play bossaball on a _____ .
3 You play underwater _____ in a swimming pool.
4 There are _____ teams in underwater hockey.
5 _____ surfing is popular in the United States.
6 There are competitions every _____ .

**Your turn!** **Think of an unusual sport.** Where do you play it? How do you play?

**Now write about it in your notebook.**

# What makes our bodies move?

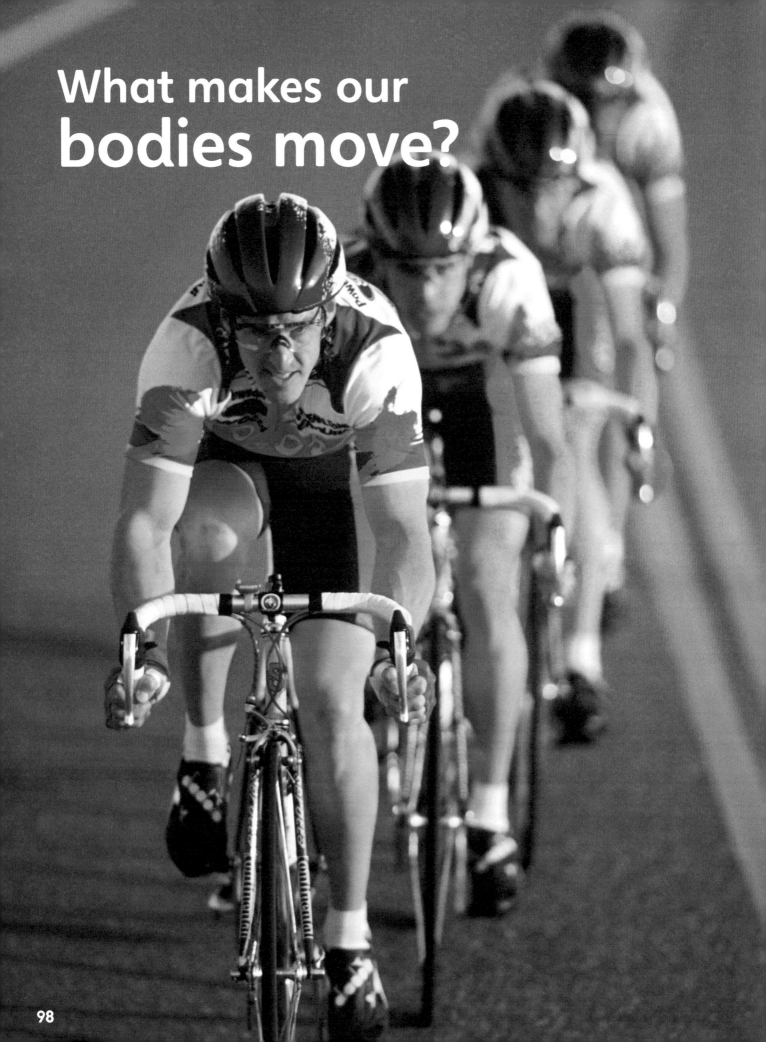

**1** 🎧 8.13 **Listen and repeat.**

| bone | muscle | knee | elbow | joint |

**2** CLIL ▶ **Watch the video.**

**3** 🎧 8.14 **Read and listen.**

We move our bodies a lot for sports because we run, jump, bend, and stretch. We use our bones, muscles, and joints.

Two or more bones meet at our joints. Elbows are joints in our arms, and knees are joints in our legs. We have lots of muscles in our body, from our faces to our feet. Muscles are connected to our bones. Muscles get longer or shorter to make our joints and bones move.

We need strong bones, muscles, and joints for sports. Some sports, like hiking, use our leg muscles. Some sports, like rowing, use our arm muscles. Some sports, like rock climbing, use leg, arm, and other muscles in our body.

**Guess What!**
We use 17 muscles in our face to smile and 43 muscles to frown!

**4** **Answer the questions.**

1 What do we use to move our bodies?
2 Where are our knee and elbow joints?
3 How do our muscles help us to move?
4 Why should our bones, muscles, and joints be strong?

**5** **Which parts of your body are the strongest and the weakest?**

**Let's collaborate!**

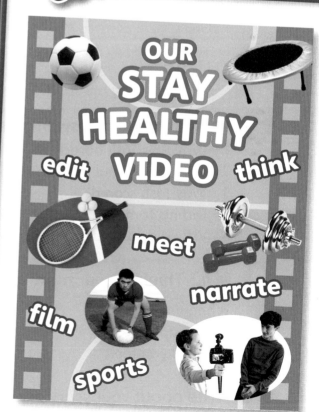

OUR STAY HEALTHY VIDEO
edit think meet narrate film sports

# Review Units 7 and 8

**1**  **Read, listen, and choose the words.**

My scariest experience was last year. I was on vacation with my parents, and we went **rock climbing/hiking** in the mountains.
I was a little **bored/excited** at first. I like **hiking/rock climbing**, but we **climbed/walked** for a long time, and we didn't see anything.
Then suddenly we saw a brown **gorilla/bear**. It was really **close to/far away** from us, but I was very **excited/scared**.
We were lucky **because/but** the **gorilla/bear** didn't see us. We turned around and **walked/ran** away. We didn't **shout/laugh** or **skip/run**.
The people at the hotel were **interested in/ surprised by** our story, but after that I didn't want to go into the mountains again. I went **rowing/ trampolining** instead.

Josh

**2** **Read again and answer the questions.**
1 Why was Josh bored?
2 Was the animal close to them?
3 Was Josh scared?
4 Did his family run away?
5 Why did Josh go trampolining the next day?

**3** **My World** **Think of your most scary experience. Ask and answer.**

When did it happen?
What happened?
How did you feel?

**4** **Write about your scary experience in your notebook.**

→ Workbook page 82

**5** Play the game.

START!

FINISH

1

2 Name six outdoor sports.

3 ___ did you go ___ weekend?

4 Name six feelings words.

5 ___ you bodyboarding yesterday?

6 You go back to the start because you're scared.

7 ___ did you do ___ night?

8 Name six sea animals.

9 You stop because you're tired. Miss a turn.

10 Name six jobs around the house.

11 When ___ you ___ rock climbing?

12 You stop because you're hungry. Miss a turn.

13 ___ are you tired?

14 Name six countries.

15 Did ___ teacher trampolining on Saturday?

16 Go forward two spaces.

17 Name six gadgets.

18 Why ___ your friend worried?

STOP

STOP

**Blue**
How many words can you remember?

**Green**
Say the missing words and ask a question.

101

# Chants

## Welcome (page 7)

 **Listen and repeat the chant.**

Where are you from?
I'm from Russia.
Are you from Russia?
No, I'm not. I'm from Spain.

Where is he from?
He's from Russia.
Is she from Russia?
No, she isn't. She's from Spain.

## Unit 1 (page 17)

 **Listen and repeat the chant.**

Are you shyer than your sister?
Yes, I am.
She's more talkative than me.
Are you smarter than your sister?
No, I'm not.
She's smarter than me.

Is your friend sportier than you?
No, he isn't.
I'm sportier than him.
Is your friend naughtier than you?
Yes, he's naughtier than me,
My friend's as naughty as can be!

## Unit 2 (page 27)

 **Listen and repeat the chant.**

We should be polite and hardworking.
We shouldn't be naughty in school!
We shouldn't laugh at others.
We should be good in school!

We should listen to our teachers.
We shouldn't be naughty in school!
We shouldn't shout in the classroom.
We should be good in school!

## Unit 3 (page 40)

 **Listen and repeat the chant.**

Which fish is the biggest?
The biggest fish, the biggest fish?
Which fish is the biggest?
I think it's a whale shark!

Which bird is the strongest?
The strongest bird, the strongest bird?
Which bird is the strongest?
I think it's the eagle!

## Unit 4 (page 49)

 **Listen and repeat the chant.**

I didn't watch TV last night.
I played a computer game.
I used my laptop last night.
She played a computer game.

I didn't play on my tablet.
I studied for a test.
I used my new e-reader.
He studied for a test.

## Unit 5 (page 62)

 **Listen and repeat the chant.**

Did you have a
nice time
On your vacation?
Yes, we did – a very
nice time
On our vacation.

Did you go on a
boat trip
On your vacation?
No, we didn't – we
swam in a lake
On our vacation.

Did you go on a picnic
On your vacation?
Yes, we did – we
ate too much
On our vacation!

## Unit 6 (page 72)

 **Listen and repeat the chant.**

Who has to collect the books?
Max does, Max does.
Who has to water the plants?
Kim does, Kim does.

Who has to feed the fish?
You do, you do!
I do? OK.
I'll feed the fish today.

## Unit 7 (page 84)

 **Listen and repeat the chant.**

Why are you tired today?
Why are you tired?
I'm tired because I stayed up late.
And now I'm very tired.

Why are you worried today?
Why are you worried?
I'm worried because the test is today.
And now I'm very worried.

## Unit 8 (page 93)

 **Listen and repeat the chant.**

Where did you go on the weekend?
I went to the beach with my friends.
We didn't go swimming or snorkeling.
We went bodyboarding instead.

Where did he go on the weekend?
He went to the beach with his friends.
They didn't go swimming or snorkeling.
They went bodyboarding instead.

# Acknowledgments

Many thanks to everyone in the excellent team at Cambridge University Press & Assessment in Spain, the UK, and India.

The authors and publishers would like to thank the following contributors:

**Blooberry Design**: concept design, cover design, book design
**Hyphen**: publishing management, page make-up
**Ann Thomson**: art direction
**Gareth Boden**: commissioned photography
**Jon Barlow**: commissioned photography
**Ian Harker**: audio recording
**John Marshall Media**: "Grammar fun" recordings
**Robert Lee, Dib Dib Dub Studios**: song and chant composition
**Vince Cross**: theme tune composition
**James Richardson**: arrangement of theme tune
**Phaebus**: "CLIL" video production
**Kiki Foster**: "Look!" video production
**Bill Smith Group**: "Grammar fun" and story animations
**Sounds Like Mike Ltd**: "Grammar Fun" video production

The authors and publishers acknowledge the following sources of copyright material and are grateful for the permissions granted. While every effort has been made, it has not always been possible to identify the sources of all the material used, or to trace all copyright holders. If any omissions are brought to our notice, we will be happy to include the appropriate acknowledgements on reprinting and in the next update to the digital edition, as applicable.

Key: U = Unit

## Photography

### The following photographs are sourced from Getty Images:

U0: Image Source; Peter Adams/The Image Bank Unreleased; Richard Sharrocks/Moment; U1: Wilfried Martin; elenaleonova, VStock LLC/Tanya Constantine; Marcus LindstrAm; Sviatlana Lazarenka/iStock/Getty Images Plus; LordRunar/iStock/Getty Images Plus; Fuse; TeguhSantosa/Moment; U2: MoreISO/iStock/Getty Images Plus; altrendo images; Alistair Berg; KidStock; Rob Friedman; Digital Vision/Photodisc; clubfoto/E+; LWA/Dann Tardif/DigitalVision; U3: Stephen Frink/Image Source; Rike_/E+; WaterFrame_eda; Westend61 - Gerald Nowak/Brand X Pictures; Bryce Flynn/Moment; Daniel Baumbach/EyeEm; Photo by Jocelyn Winwood, NZ. Specialist in nature shots/Moment Open; MR1805/iStock/Getty Images Plus; joebelanger; FredFroese/iStock/Getty Images Plus; paulafrench/iStock/Getty Images Plus; Nichols801/iStock/Getty Images Plus; kali9/E+; Carol Yepes/Moment Open; JulPo/iStock/Getty Images Plus; Csondy/iStock/Getty Images Plus; U4: Phimph Ma Yexa/EyeEm; Tara Farquhar/EyeEm; baranozdemir/iStock/Getty Images Plus; U5: Photography by Byron Tanaphol Prukston/Moment; Fox3X; Renata Habibullina/EyeEm; Corey Ford/Stocktrek Images; Douglas Peebles/Corbis Documentary; O. Louis Mazzatenta; U6: Jupiterimages/The Image Bank; WLADIMIR BULGAR/Science Photo Library; Petri Oeschger/E+; Barry Austin Photography/The Image Bank; MIXA; SolStock/E+; John Coletti/The Image Bank; SCStock/iStock Editorial; U7: DigitalVision/Getty;Peter Dazeley/The Image Bank; Jose Luis Pelaez Inc/DigitalVision; chuanchai/iStock/Getty Images Plus; I love nature/Moment; U8: mountainberryphoto/iStock/Getty Images Plus; Tom Werner/DigitalVision; Blend Images - Michael DeYoung/Tetra images; John P Kelly.

### The following photographs are sourced from other libraries:

U0: Tim Gainey/Alamy; Charnsit Ramyarupa/Shutterstock; Globe Turner/Shutterstock; Paul Stringer/Shutterstock; Media Home/Shutterstock; Artgraphixel/Shutterstock; Tanya Ustenko/Shutterstock; Sporrer/Rupp/Image Source/Alamy; Radius Images/Design Pics/Alamy; RimDream/Shutterstock; Ekaterina Bykova/Shutterstock; Christine Whitehead/Alamy; SandiMako/Shutterstock; ANDRE DURAO/Shutterstock; Jose Luis Pelaez Inc/Tetra Images, LLC/Alamy; Ekaterina Bykova/Shutterstock; Norman Price/Alamy; marekuliasz/Shutterstock; Destinyweddingstudio/Shutterstock; dbimages/Alamy; BRYANT Nicolas/SAGAPHOTO.COM/Alamy; U1: Menzl Guenter/Shutterstock; Amir Kaljikovic/Shutterstock; Ian Allenden/Alamy; ZouZou/Shutterstock; Przemek Klos/Shutterstock; Shots Studio/Shutterstock; WEExp/Shutterstock; Vasilyev Alexandr/Shutterstock; Anneka/Shutterstock; Q-Images/Alamy; Nick Turner/Alamy; imageBROKER/Alamy; Philippe Degroote/Alamy; elic/Shutterstock; noolwlee/Shutterstock; Johner Images/Corbis; pattara puttiwong/Shutterstock; EyeEm/Alamy; National Geographic Image Collection/Alamy; U2: J. McPhail/Shutterstock; Purestock/Alamy; iofoto/
Shutterstock; MJTH/Shutterstock; Peter Alvey/Alamy; Cultura Creative/Alamy; Tom Wang/Shutterstock; Werli Francois/Alamy; syaochka/Shutterstock; Jon Bower UK/Alamy; David Bathgate/Corbis; Sergey Borisov/Alamy; billy bonns/Shutterstock; U3: Steve Noakes/Shutterstock; Kevin Schafer/Shutterstock; Stefan Pircher/Shutterstock; imageBROKER/Alamy; Nature Picture Library/Alamy; Christian Musat/Alamy; Nick Upton/Alamy; Zac Macaulay/Cultura RM/Alamy; Stefan Deutsch/Corbis; Carlos Villoch - MagicSea.com/Alamy; Artem Rudik/Shutterstock; U4: Dimple Bhati/iStock/Getty Images Plus; FERNANDO BLANCO CALZADA/Shutterstock; Jiri Hera/Shutterstock; K. Miri Photography/Shutterstock; keellla/Shutterstock; Valentina Razumova/Shutterstock; neelsky/Shutterstock; Maxx- Studio/Shutterstock; Tara Farquhar / EyeEm; Igor Lateci/Shutterstock; Julien_N/Shutterstock; dpa picture alliance/Alamy; Gordon Scammell/Alamy; Goodluz/Shutterstock; Blend Images/Alamy; baranozdemir/iStock/Getty Images Plus; INTERFOTO/Alamy; Magnavox Corporation/Science and Society Picture Library; Chris Willson/Alamy; Darwin Wiggett/All Canada Photos/Alamy; Ale Ventura/Corbis; U5: Galyna Andrushko/Shutterstock; Pablo Hidalgo - Fotos593/Shutterstock; Andrea Willmore/Shutterstock; Filip Fuxa/Shutterstock; Chris Gardiner/Shutterstock; Dr. Morley Read/Shutterstock; lenaer/Shutterstock; Janne Hamalainen/Shutterstock; VVO/Shutterstock; Drimi/Shutterstock; javarman/Shutterstock; Robert Hoetink/Shutterstock; holbox/Shutterstock; orangecrush/Shutterstock; Eugene Sergeev/Alamy; Four Oaks/Shutterstock; Eric Nathan/Alamy; Rolf Nussbaumer Photography/Alamy; Martin Harvey/Alamy; Anthony Bannister/Avalon.red/Alamy; kkaplin/Shutterstock; WhyMePhoto/Shutterstock; Florapix/Alamy; Rolf Nussbaumer Photography/Alamy; Image Source/Alamy; Nordroden/Shutterstock; Tamara Kulikova/Shutterstock; wdeon/Shutterstock; luigi nifosi/Shutterstock; U6: John Birdsall/Rex; Arina P Habich/Shutterstock; Blend Images/Shutterstock; MBI/Alamy; Shotshop GmbH/Alamy; Juice Images/Alamy; tmcphotos/Shutterstock; Monkey Business Images/Shutterstock; The Photolibrary Wales/Alamy; Sergio Pitamitz/robertharding/Alamy; Aflo Co. Ltd./Alamy; Lukasz Janyst/Shutterstock; Andrey Starostin/Shutterstock; Aksenova Natalya/Shutterstock; Kletr/Shutterstock; Rob Swanson/Shutterstock; Bucchi Francesco/Shutterstock; U7: blickwinkel/Alamy; PathDoc/Shutterstock; Thinglass/Shutterstock; Scott E Read/Shutterstock; Martin Harvey/Alamy; Maria Dryfhout/Shutterstock; Muythaisong Pitakpong/Shutterstock; U8: Dimitar Kunev/Shutterstock; Zero Creative/Image Source/Alamy; stephen brian/Alamy; Robin Weaver/Alamy; imageBROKER/Alamy; Catchlight Visual Services/Alamy; BlueOrange Studio/Shutterstock; Arterra Picture Library/Alamy; Max Topchii/Shutterstock; Charles Hood/Alamy; ALAN OLIVER/Alamy; Blend Images/Alamy; Brocreative/Shutterstock; Radius Images/Alamy; RODRIGO OROPEZA/Corbis; Patryk Kosmider/Shutterstock; Matyas Rehak/Shutterstock; RODRIGO OROPEZA/Corbis; Sebastian Kaulitzki/Shutterstock; leonello calvetti/Alamy; Image Source/Alamy; BlueRing_Boumy/Shutterstock; All Canada Photos/Alamy.

Front Cover Photography by areeya_ann/500px Plus.

## Illustrations

Graham Kennedy; Mark Duffin; Marcus Cutler (Sylvie Poggio); Pablo Gallego (Beehive Illustration).